STUCK ON
1/FO
RTY

STUCK ON 1/FORTY. PRITISH NANDY

A NEW COLLECTION OF POEMS.

AMARYLLIS

AMARYLLIS

This edition first published 2012

AMARYLLIS

Editorial Office:
J-39, Ground Floor, Jor Bagh Lane,
New Delhi 110 003, India
Tel: 011-24642447/24652447 Fax: 011-24622448
Email: amaryllis@amaryllis.co.in
Website: www.amaryllis.co.in

Registered Office:
10, Nishat Colony, Bhopal 462 003, M.P., India

ISBN: 978-93-81506-20-2

Designed by:
Rangita Pritish Nandy
Ishita Pritish Nandy

Printed and Bound in India by:
Thomson Press (India) Ltd.

Difficult, whimsical, impossible at times
for Ishita, my daughter
without whom every book I write would be incomplete.

Books by Pritish Nandy

Poetry

Of Gods & Olives (Calcutta/ Mexico City, 1967)
On Either Side of Arrogance (Calcutta, 1968)
I Hand You In Turn My Nebbuk Wreath (Calcutta, 1968)
From the Outer Bank of the Brahmaputra (New York, 1969)
Masks to be Interpreted in Terms of Messages (Calcutta, 1971)
Madness is the Second Stroke (Calcutta, 1972)
The Poetry of Pritish Nandy: Collected Poems (New Delhi, 1973)
Riding the Midnight River: Selected Poems (New Delhi/ London, 1974)
Dhritarashtra Downtown: Zero (Calcutta, 1974)
Collected Poems (Calcutta, 1973)
Lonesong Street (Calcutta, 1975)
In Secret Anarchy (Calcutta, 1976)
The Nowhere Man (Calcutta, 1976)
A Stranger Called I (Calcutta, 1976)
Tonight, This Savage Rite/ With Kamala Das (New Delhi, 1977)
Anywhere is Another Place (Calcutta, 1979)
Pritish Nandy 30 (Calcutta, 1980)
The Rainbow Last Night (New Delhi, 1981)
Again (New Delhi, 2010)
Tonight, This Savage Rite/ With Kamala Das/ Reissued with drawings by Manu Parekh (New Delhi, 2011)

Verse Play

Rites for a Plebeian Statue (Calcutta, 1970)

Short Stories

Some Friends (Calcutta, 1979)

Translations

The Complete Poems of Samar Sen (Calcutta, 1970)
Subhas Mukhopadhyay: Poet of the People (Calcutta, 1970)
Poems from Bangladesh (Calcutta, 1971)
The Prose Poems of Lokenath Bhattacharya (Calcutta, 1971)
Bangladesh: Voice of a New Nation with drawings by Feliks Topolski (Calcutta/ London/ New York, 1972)
Shesh Lekha: The Last Poems of Tagore (Calcutta, 1973)
Modern Bengali Poetry (Chicago, 1974)
The Flaming Giraffe: Poems by Sunil Gangopadhyay (Calcutta, 1975)
Songs of Mirabai (New Delhi, 1975)
The Poetry of Kaifi Azmi (Calcutta, 1975)
Krishna, Krishna: Poems by Kabir (New Delhi, 1976)
The Lord is my Shepherd (New Delhi, 1982)
Untamed Heart: Poems by Bhartrhari with drawings by Samir Mondal (New Delhi, 1994)
Unchained Melody: Poems by Amaru with drawings by Samir Mondal (New Delhi, 1994)
Careless Whispers: Sanskrit Love Poetry with drawings by MF Husain (New Delhi, 1994)
Shesh Lekha: The Last Poems of Tagore/ Reissued with paintings by Paresh Maity (New Delhi, 2011)

Poetry Recordings

Lonesong Street, with Ananda Shankar (EMI, 1977)
Hazaaron Khwaishein Aisi, with Shantanu Moitra (Virgin, 2004)

In Bengali Translation

Pritish Nandyr Kobita translated by Amarendra Chakravarti (Calcutta, 1975)
Pritish Nandyr Kobita translated by Shakti Chattopadhyay (Calcutta, 1978)

Anthologies Edited

Indian Poetry in English: 1947-1972 (Calcutta, 1972)
Indian Poetry in English Today (New Delhi, 1973)
Modern Indian Poetry (New Delhi/ London, 1974)
Modern Indian Love Poetry (New Delhi, 1974)
Modern Indian Love Stories (New Delhi, 1974)
Strangertime (New Delhi, 1976)

...and in the end, the love you take is equal to the love you make.

John Lennon

Why poetry?

I fell in love with words when I was young, very young. In fact, long before I even fell in love with a girl. I felt that words could not only convey what I wanted to say, what I felt, what I sought, what I wondered at, but they could also heal, touch, reason with me, reach out to others, stumble, fall, rise again. Words were my best friends, my adversaries, my lovers who occasionally betrayed me. I would fence with them like D'Artagnon. I would grapple with them in the dark like Jacob grappled with the Angel of Death. I would seek their companionship in my loneliest moments.

And thus was born my poetry.

I began to write poetry before I learnt to write prose. And I wrote many books of poems, most of which I no longer possess. They were published by small publishers and university presses. They were translated into other languages. Some of them were set to music, published as record albums. Short films were made on them.

And then, suddenly one day, in my mid-twenties, something within me snapped. Without any explanation to anyone, including myself, I abandoned the solipsistic, self indulgent world of poetry and turned to prose, prose that I hoped could help me change the world around me. I guess the Emergency had something to do with it. I felt angry, betrayed. So I gave up the starkness of poetry, the frugality, the battle with words and images and switched over to journalism. I wrote millions of words over the next two decades in the hope that I could make a difference to my city, my country, my people. I became a chronicler of my times. Sometimes joyous, most times enraged but never bitter. Faith kept me going.

It still does. I believe in India. I believe that what we write, what we say, what we capture on the screen can make a great difference. And that's why I write, make movies, paint, create. All that I do is born out of the conviction that people eventually listen to the voice of reason. Compassion always has its way. I believe that if more people chose to love each other rather than the latest sports car, yacht or handbag, the world would be an infinitely better place. But I have also realised that my beliefs, however strongly held, can't change the world, and may be that is a good thing. An imperfect world is a far more interesting place to live in. But yes, each one of us, whether it's Hitler or Gandhi, Mother Teresa or Osama bin Laden or that unknown homeless man who sits outside Haji Ali, leave our footprints on the streets we walk, so that those who come after us can remember the good we do and ignore the bad.

Meanwhile, words are changing. So is language. The epics have yielded way to shorter, quicker, smarter books. Homer and Valmiki bow before Lady Gaga today, as she engages with her 20 million followers on Twitter in a new dialect where 140 characters can say more than the fattest book. The comma and the semi colon have retired. So have Wren and Martin. I just gave away half my library to fund an NGO that looks after stray dogs on Mumbai's streets. But the urgency of language remains intact. So does the power and the passion of words. In fact, never before in history have words acquired greater importance than today simply because no one has the time any more for asterisks and footnotes.

You just get that one shot at immortality. If your words fail you, it's gone.

So I am back to poetry. It's different from what I have written before. But it addresses the same concerns, and in many ways the same issues because the more the world changes, the more it remains the same. We seek the same things, pursue the same dreams, ask the same questions in different ways today. We cope with the same tedious successes. And we grapple bravely with the same glorious failures.

The poems here are for those who enjoy the magic of words, who believe that an image conjured by words can be as powerful, as moving as one captured by a Nikon DSLR, who still argue that three words strung together with the impassioned glue of hope can change the world. You can read these poems. You can look at them. You can tweet them. (For no poem crosses 140 characters.) You can even whisper them, gently and sensuously, to those you love.

As for me, I simply write them because I know of no other way to fight this boring sense of mortality.

Pritish Nandy/ March 9, 2012

STUCK ON 1/FORTY

I pause too often.

Delete.

Start my life all over again.

Am I God

or the eternal Fool?

Sex is sexier at my age.

So is rage. Let's try again

my queen of Spain.
This time, in the rain.

Cities come and go.

Bombay is Mumbai now.

Calcutta, Kolkata.

Where will I hide from you

or for that matter

from myself? **I write me**

a passport to hell.

Be decisive.
Let me go.

It doesn't really matter where I go

as long as it's
far from you and me.

An entire continent
grows
around this single poem:

I am startled
by my own silences.

Speak.

Write me a poem
one day
without words:
she said.

So I went to you.
You told me to go away.

There was never much time
to tell you where
I came from,
where I went
that night

when I missed you
and the dark came tumbling down.

Emptiness grows

when music plays and

words fall apart.

They scatter across

the skies

like frightened gulls.

I grew up with dragonflies.

You gifted me a dragon.

In the dungeons
of my solitude
grew this strange wordplay.

Say it once more
and I will come away
to where the green
and gold play

in this faithless sunset.

Scrabble me a name

that fame

did not spoil.

So why blame me alone

for this luckless soul?

Stop me now,
before I leave this empty space
and grow
black roses

in the backyard of your home.

Alone.

I am empty now.
Turn over. Go to sleep.

Let me
count
my
sheep

till day breaks
with the chatter of silences.

I left you behind
and came to this city
catching
nowhere in the rain.

Call me back
where I belong,
return me my unfinished song.

Every time
I try to get lost
the unknown street I take
finds its way
back to you.

Is it me
or is it you today
who is lost?

Accost me
with colours I have never seen,
words I have never heard,
loves I have never known

and I will show you
where the rainbow ends
tonight.

Love is more easily said
than done.
Passion's quicker.

Lust
flickers

like a luckless candle in the wind.
It's a scandal.

I have cheated you many, many times. Worse, I have cheated on myself

with words, words that meant nothing to either of us.

Every time
you said nothing to me
I knew exactly
what you meant.

It's only when
you spoke
that I misunderstood you.

Night's the only time
miracles happen:
you and I
suddenly become we

and we
becomes me
that much more easily.

Antelopes run
through the forests
of time:

is it you
I make love to
or is it me?
Do we really know?
Do we care?

Are we blind in the dark?
Why do we grope
for bodies
we know so well?

Why do we seek
redemption in
just another fuck?

Dark waters of hell

wash away our pain,

the blinding rain

calls out to us again:

Wildflowers sing

in Ibiza.

Let's go.

We circle each other

grappling

with the idea

of bringing each other

down, on the mat.

Sex is a bit

like wrestling,

at least to begin with.

But that's where
all resemblances end.
The guns come out
blazing thereafter.

**Assassins
take over
the stage.**

Tempt me.

Coax me.

Seduce me.

Win me back again.

This is where I was,
am,
but just a little bored.

I am my own assassin.
In the crosshairs
of my gun
I see only me.

Some day I will pull

the trigger.

Will you miss me?

I have spent

an entire lifetime

whoring with words,

images,

secret moments

spent with eternity.

You are
where I want to be.

Insolent, angry

wicked: that's me

or so you say

before you angrily

look away.

Faith is so yesterday.

Tomorrow

is where I want to be.

Audacity is what I begin with.

That's my usual entry point.

The rest comes later.
Love. Belonging.
Take away.

What binds us together
is this insolence.
The world belongs to us,
to do as we wish.

**Destroy it or
piece it together–
all over again.**

There's no one here
I know but you:
This planet doesn't belong to us.
Stars whiz around.
Meteors too.

**Let's catch a spaceship
back home.**

The Mahatma left me
a legacy. The rest came more
easily. Books, art, movies,
the huntdown of truth.

Restless enemies.
A timeless search
for nothing at all.

We began with nothing.

A casual glance across a room
teeming with people
neither of us knew

or wanted to.

Our eyes locked.
A smile, and thus began
this journey.

Words like love
sound funny when your nose
is running, your eyes
bloodshot, fever's high.

**Reassurance
is no way
to show you need me.**

I have backpacked my way
down lonely highways,
slept in unfamiliar rooms,
picked up rides
with strangers till I met you

my enemy, my friend,
my lover.

This poem
comes back to me
like an unposted letter

a scribble
that I can never read.
Unsigned.

Where shall we meet
if not there
where the sea
and the sky merge

like a solemn promise
of eternity?

A murmur of wind
and rain
rises like fever

if you ever return

I will rise like Lazarus
to your touch.

Follow the sun
through rain

darkness
solitude
pain

follow it

till it drops
into the sea, disappears.

You lie. So do I.

Does that make us liars?

Or are we just lovers

claiming

our share

of eternity?

Were we to pause
and reconsider
perhaps this love
would be a lie.

Let's try
to make it real.

Inside the hotel

stood white columns

washed by the sea

white gulls screamed

at the starched sky.

Naked

under the rainbow

you lay:

tomorrow

is just another day.

Maybe quieter.

Eyes closed.
Rivers turn in,
skies race across
the clouds,
night trips over, falls

into my arms.

Memory reinvents
the past,
tomorrow unfolds its legs:

I see you somewhere

**lurching
into
eternity**

Forests are always crowded

with nothing

in particular, apart from fear

It's just like the way

we are:

stoned

by our own memories.

On a scarred afternoon

I write these lines for you

wherever you may be

I hope

I may break into a dream or two

I return from the edge
dark with pain
and emptiness

this is no place
to burn your shadow:
if you must
go fret somewhere else.

There are not many places
to hide
even if you don't want to.

It's easier to stand out
in the sun

and burn,
burn yourself out.

Your laughter

eagerly wakes me up
to a morning
broken by the sounds
of nothingness:

down the road
is the Fontana di Trevi.

I like the way Hemingway went.

Was he cleaning his gun
or seeking redemption
from an ageing God

who simply refused to listen?

Many of them
had husbands, lovers, friends
and I knew them all.

Yet it was charming
to urge them to stray, away
from these ties
and pursue love.

I have no memory of my birth.

I can't predict
when I shall die.

All I know is
I have spent these years in between
like a king.

How dark were those nights
of endless passion
when we never saw
each other's face

**and yet stroked each other
to sleep before the day broke?**

Did you say Rampur?
I have been there before
with you,
sat under starlit skies,
driven through long endless nights

and declared my love for you.

Days end, nights begin

the snows of Kilimanjaro melt
each time
our bodies seek each other out

like words of a poem
falling in place.

Poems are never about words.

You reach inside

a forgotten memory,

revive it

part lie,

part truth

and piece it together

convincingly.

We picked up maps in London

drove to the

past life regression therapist

who lived

nowhere in particular

and found nothing

that mattered.

DC
was cold.

Bush had just delivered his speech.
To each, his own.

We walked out
to catch the wind in our sails.
On just another
February morning.

I grew up with Banalata Sen

watching isles of spice
rise through the restless waters
of seas I never saw

anywhere
but in your eyes

Most cities I never remember
most loves
I have left behind.

Remind me
that you once existed
remind me
our love never died.

These streets were never mine,

these homes
these shadows
of times long gone

I am torn between memory
and wilful amnesia.

Shut the door.
Keep all that I cannot
and will not remember
out.

Just
shout out
my name

and I will knock again.

The road outside our house
was named after
a poem I wrote for someone else.

But you gave birth
to our children here:
In this hierarchy of pain.

Every morning
the blue bus stumbled down
the broken roads
of Howrah

till I reached the factory
and found that nothing really
mattered but you.

The dark blue waters
in the grotto:
the boat from Naples
still reverberates

with the sounds of music.

Stations whiz by.

So do memories of people,
loves, fears,
places we have never been to.

There are no tickets
on the train to nowhere.

At night
we sometimes pause,
catch our breath

say words we do not mean
to each other.

Is love a lie

or just another way to say
we will not die?

The sun sets
on the waterfront gently,
almost too gently
for you and I.

Shall we settle down in Nice
or return home
once it's all over?

Why am I on twitter?

Do I need friends all over again?

Or am I hunting down
my solitudes one by one?

The inky blue sky of Provence
is still swept by gulls.

Ravi Shankar's theme
from Pather Panchali
gently plays on my iPod.

**When did I
lose my
childhood?**

Sartre's gone.
So has Camus.

Paz returned home
never to come back again.

All I have for company is
Baudelaire's Fleurs du Mal.

I love you more

every time I meet you

and sometimes

even more when I don't.

The darbari kannada

contexts the moment:

the gull swoops down

to pick its prey.

The catamaran cuts through
the bay, a ray
of sunshine announces dusk.

**A moment
sliced
out of time.**

A sudden swish through the air:

the nihonto
is but a weapon of my desire.

Night gently drops on us like a veil.

There is gunfire outside,
people screaming,
roads running away.

I shall miss you more when
these wars end.

Love is not as easy

as it sounds.

Sex is bewildering.

What remains is

but a fistful of memories

chucked in the rain.

At school I learnt
minuets, polonaises, quadrilles.
Hayden, Mozart, Beethoven
preoccupied me.

And you, yes
you and I waltzing through the night.

On the coast of Capri
Grotta Azzurra:
just you and me
and the sun reflecting
off the waters

where shall we be
when we leave Capri?

The tramcar hurtles

through the night,

Kolkata sleeps

as I walk alone

alone in the dark, through

lonely parks

to where I want to be.

Zatoichi the blind swordsman
catches me unaware.

And as I fall
like an autumn leaf
you come from nowhere.

It's been a long journey
from Cadiz to Gibraltar
on a shipwreck of dreams.

**It's time to
pause, rest
then sail again
against the rain.**

Why

is life worth living?

There are many answers

short and long

many questions,

almost all wrong.

Tracey's face cuts

to a Manhattan montage.

There is nothing

I have loved more than you

my country.

Yet there's no one

who has hurt me more than you.

I bring you nothing more

than these torn sheets of paper

and memories wafting

in the warm summer breeze

of times forgotten.

Lost

in the impermanence
of everything I watch

I wait, restless

for you to write me a story

that none shall read.

Of all the colours I saw
your laughter
was the brightest
in summer

red, blue, yellow, white:
right,
I am startled by
this intimacy of the night.

I write the last chapter
of my unfinished novel:

you are part
of my unfinished life

seeking closure.

Every person here,

every moment, every joy

and pain and celebration

makes us whole:

you are me,
my country

and I? Nobody but you.

You surround me

with your warm, wet summer love.

I enter you slyly

as I would my home,

after a long absence.

On tip toes.

It is night.

The right time to seek you out

wherever you may be.

Within me
or without.

Out somewhere in the dark.

I know nothing about mathematics

except you and I
make we, and we equals infinity.

Poetry is our break time.

Highways are best in the dark

You never get lost.

In the glare of my headlights

I stare at nothing

as starlight beats down on me

as rain.

I wake up to nothing every morning

but you.

The day creates itself around me.

I lurch between
extremes

:is God
drunk?

Or are these constellations
under my feet?

The croupier deals
me a dud

it doesn't really matter
when

you keep
winning.

Battles I never lost.

It's the war that outwits me.

You, God, me:
this tiresome threesome
can never win.

I open the newspaper
every morning
to read my own obit.

It’s funny

how much fun living is.

STUCK ON

1/FO

RTY